LISTENING IS *an* ACT *of* LOVE

. . . . . .

Notes on Ten Beloved Stories—and
How to Record Your Own

. . . . . .

THE PENGUIN PRESS

New York

2007

Penguin Audio
*Listening Is an Act of Love: Ten Beloved Stories
from the StoryCorps Project*
Narrated and with an introduction by Dave Isay

Listening Is an Act of Love is available in hardcover from The Penguin Press.
Total playing time: 36:33 minutes
© 2007 StoryCorps
℗ 2007 Penguin Audio, a member of Penguin Group (USA) Inc.
All rights reserved.

Penguin Audio is a member of Penguin Group (USA) Inc.
375 Hudson Street
New York, N.Y. 10014

Designed by Amanda Dewey

Manufactured in Mexico
$7.00 suggested retail price
www.penguin.com

Listening Is an Act of Love
Ten Beloved Stories from the StoryCorps Project
NARRATED AND WITH AN INTRODUCTION BY DAVE ISAY

TRACK LIST

• • •

1. DANNY PERASA, 65, speaking with his wife, ANNIE, 61

RECORDED IN NEW YORK, NEW YORK, AND BROOKLYN, NEW YORK

In 2004, a few months after StoryCorps opened its first booth in Grand Central Station, Danny and Annie Perasa made the trip by subway from Brooklyn. He worked as a clerk at Off-Track Betting; she was a nurse. They had come to the booth because they wanted to document their twenty-five-year-long love affair. They brought with them a stack of love letters they'd written to each other over the years.

It would be hard to imagine two people more in love than Danny and Annie. Every morning, Danny would write Annie a love letter and leave it on the kitchen table for her to find when she got up. They embodied so much of what StoryCorps is about—the eloquence, power, grace and poetry in the words of everyday people; the notion that the lives of the people we pass walking down the street can be as compelling as—even more compelling than—those of the rich and famous.

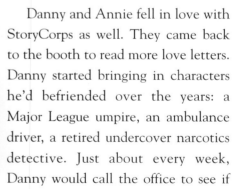

Danny and Annie fell in love with StoryCorps as well. They came back to the booth to read more love letters. Danny started bringing in characters he'd befriended over the years: a Major League umpire, an ambulance driver, a retired undercover narcotics detective. Just about every week, Danny would call the office to see if we wanted him or Annie to visit the booth. "I had a cataract operation over the weekend. Do you need me to come in and talk about it?"

Listeners around the country fell in love with Danny and Annie, too, and they became the unofficial spokespeople for StoryCorps. Danny and Annie never ceased to astound listeners with their kindness, humor, wisdom and, most of all, their boundless love for each other.

In January 2006, Danny was diagnosed with end-stage pancreatic cancer. That February StoryCorps renamed the Grand Central booth in honor of him and Annie. A week later, too sick to travel to the booth, Danny asked StoryCorps to come to his house in Bay Ridge, Brooklyn, to record one last conversation with Annie. They recorded that interview on a  Thursday. It aired on NPR the next Friday. Danny passed away two hours after the broadcast. E-mails flooded into NPR's Web site. In all, Annie received close to fifteen hundred condolence letters from StoryCorps listeners. At Danny's funeral, Annie carried a copy of these letters in her arms and placed them inside the casket to be buried with him. She kept a second copy at home. She continues to read one of these condolence letters each day instead of her daily love note from Danny.

January 6, 2006, and February 16, 2006

2. JUDGE JOE PIGOTT, 81, interviewed by his wife, LORRAINE, 76

RECORDED IN JACKSON, MISSISSIPPI

Judge Joe Pigott came into a StoryBooth in Jackson, Mississippi, with his wife, Lorraine, to talk about their lives together. But the story here is from their life apart—from Joe's working life behind the bench as a judge. He was a circuit court judge in the Fourteenth Judicial District for eighteen years and before that he worked as a prosecutor and district attorney, all in the state of Mississippi.

When Lorraine asks Joe to reminisce about his career, what comes first to mind is a man named Willie Earl "Pip" Dow, an incorrigible small-time thief who always managed to make the judge laugh. Pip had two bad habits: drinking and stealing to pay for his drinking. He and Judge Pigott saw each other so many times that they built up a relationship of sorts, a kind of mutual respect.

Still, Pip always found a way of one-upping the judge. He made a surprise appearance at Joe's retirement ceremony, where they were hanging his portrait at the courthouse. It seemed an odd thing for Pip

 to do, considering the number of years in jail he had spent at Joe's order, but he said, "Well, I heard they were going to hang Judge Pigott at the courtroom and so I didn't want to miss that."

January 27, 2007

3. PEGGY EDWARDS, 81, interviewed by her granddaughter, CINEMA WOOD, 32

RECORDED IN WASHINGTON, D.C.

Cinema Wood wanted to capture her grandmother's voice on tape and get her advice on marriage. So she brought her grandmother Peggy Edwards into a StoryCorps booth in Washington, D.C., and asked her to tell the story of meeting "Papa," Cinema's grandfather G. Franklin Edwards. Franklin was teaching at Howard University in Washington, D.C., where Peggy was working as a secretary. It was 1946.

> *"I love you,*
> *oh I just love you."*

They met by chance—she happened to be filling in for a few weeks at the registrar's office at Howard, and he happened to be visiting from Chicago, where he was working on a doctorate. He kept staring at her legs, and she was indignant. "Pardon me, sir, what is your name?" But his impertinence got something started—after six months, they decided to marry. When Franklin passed away in 1998, they had been married for fifty-two years, and as Peggy remembers it, they had only good times together. Franklin finished graduate school and returned to teach at Howard; Peggy worked in her family's funeral home on U Street. They had one daughter, Cinema's mother, Donalee. As a grandmother, Peggy is effusive: "I love you, oh I just love you. From the moment you were born!"

Peggy gave Cinema, who was about to get married, some sage advice on marriage—"Go slow. It's not a marathon; it's just a stroll."

May 20, 2005

4. DAN E. ANDREWS, JR., 84,
interviewed by his daughter,
MARY McCORMICK, 57

Mary McCormick brought her father, Dan Andrews, into the StoryBooth when it was near their homes in San Diego, California. She wanted to record his memories of growing up in Lawton, Oklahoma, during the Great Depression. Despite the hardships, Dan remembered his childhood fondly. He was, in Mary's words, "a very enterprising child," one who found many ways to earn a few coins here and there. He sold magazines and newspapers, collected empty bottles and gathered scrap metal. But here, Dan remembers the scariest memory of his enterprising youth.

> *"And suddenly we could feel the tracks shaking, and we heard the train whistle."*

In the very early years of the Depression, Dan collected coal from railroad tracks, where it fell from passing trains as engineers scooped madly to keep the coal engines running at full steam. Those scraps could be gathered together for much needed heat—people were desperately poor, and it was a particularly frigid winter. The tracks ran just seven blocks from his parents' house, and the boys knew them pretty well. But one day, when Dan, his friend Joe and Joe's kid brother decided to go looking for coal on the tracks, they made a terrible miscalculation about the train schedule. Dan saved the day, but he

shies away from accolades: "It wasn't about being a hero, it was just about being kids and not understanding the danger."

Dan's scare that day didn't keep him from continuing to use his ingenuity. As he said in his interview, "I mean, a lot of people run away from work, but it's really fun to work. So that's kind of been my philosophy. I've tried to stay busy all day."

February 20, 2006

5. SARAH LITTMAN, 42, interviewed by her son, JOSHUA, 12

RECORDED IN NEW YORK, NEW YORK

Sarah Littman's partner for her StoryCorps conversation was younger than most: her son, Joshua, who was only twelve at the time. But Joshua's questions were among the most poignant, probing and creative ever heard in a StoryCorps booth. Joshua was diagnosed with Asperger's syndrome—a form of autism—when he was five. He was born in England and moved to Connecticut with his mother and younger sister, Amie, in 1999. When Joshua came to the StoryBooth, he was in the seventh grade and an honor's student, but his Asperger's makes socializing difficult for him.

In their interview, Joshua asked a series of remarkable questions of his mother. One characteristic of Asperger's syndrome is a tendency to become obsessed with a single area of interest—for Joshua it's animals. But, as Sarah let him know, their exceptional conversations have made her a better mother. "I really had to learn to think out of the box with you. And it's made me much more creative, as a parent and as a person. And I'll always thank you for that."

 Sarah made Joshua a binder of the letters he received from public radio listeners after the broadcast of his story, so that when he's feeling down he can look at the letters and feel supported.

February 23, 2006

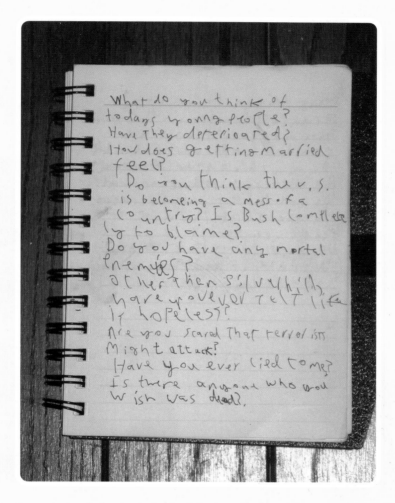

Joshua's notebook of questions for his mother

6. DR. LYNN WEAVER, 58,
interviewed by his daughter,
KIMBERLY, 37

When Lynn Weaver came into a StoryCorps Griot booth in Atlanta, Georgia, he told his daughter, Kimberly, about his father, Thurman Weaver, a factory worker, chauffeur and World War II veteran. Lynn remembers his father as his rock—the person he would go to with any question or problem.

Lynn grew up in Knoxville, Tennessee, at a time when the schools were being desegregated.

"I would be a success if my children loved me half as much as I loved my father."

The environment was such that he recalls, "there were many times when I was just scared." He felt safe as soon as he saw his father.

Kimberly has often heard her father say that her mother is the smartest person he knows, but he points out his father was equally brilliant.

He remembers the time that his father stayed up all night teaching himself algebra so he could then teach it to his son the next day.

After hearing his story played at a StoryCorps event in Atlanta, Lynn wrote a letter to StoryCorps:

* * *

You will never know how honored and touched I was by the playing of the remembrance of my dad. After I got home, I realized that the evening of the reception was the anniversary of my father's death. Even in death, he continues to embrace me with his love.

Lynn Weaver, MD
Chairman of Surgery
Morehouse School of Medicine
Atlanta, Georgia

February 24, 2007

7. ELAINE LEINUNG, 50, speaking with her husband, JOHN, 51

RECORDED IN NEW YORK, NEW YORK

StoryCorps has been collecting September 11th interviews in a special initiative begun in 2005. Elaine Leinung and her husband, John, came in to remember their son, Paul Battaglia. Paul died in the attacks on the World Trade Center, where he worked at Marsh & McLennan as a risk consultant. Like many families remembering loved ones killed in the attacks, they spent much of the interview talking about Paul as a child. Paul was John's stepson, but he first met John at age two. By the time of Paul's first communion, around age seven, he was calling him Dad. Paul's family ties were very strong. They remember his sister Kristen's adoration of her brother—how she would protect him, "Leave my Paul alone." The family was soon to get bigger—the night before the attacks, the Leinungs had been discussing Paul's upcoming engagement to his girlfriend.

It was important for the Leinungs to remember together the day of the attacks and how it was that they came to realize they had lost their beloved son, who was only twenty-two years old.

Since that day, they have started two scholarships in his name,

 one at his high school and one at Binghamton University, his alma mater. As Elaine told John in the interview, "It's a deep sadness that just won't ever completely leave."

March 22, 2005

8. GRETE MEERHOLZ, 40, speaking with her husband, KEITH, 39

RECORDED IN NEW YORK, NEW YORK

Keith Meerholz and his wife, Grete, also came into the StoryCorps booth to remember the events of September 11, 2001. Keith worked at Marsh & McClennan. He was on an express elevator to his hundredth-floor office when the first plane hit. Keith made it out of the towers alive. Grete watched the towers fall on television and was convinced that her husband had perished. When Keith finally called her she screamed to let everyone who had gathered know that he was alive.

> *"It's nice to have a best friend to go through life with."*

At times, Grete says, they'll disagree or get angry with each other. And then, Grete tells Keith, she remembers how she almost lost him on that day, "and I can kind of forgive you for anything." Laughter keeps them going, too. Grete tells Keith, "I love you because you make me laugh, and you're my best friend And it's nice to have a best friend to go through life with."

April 4, 2005

9. PRIYA MORGANSTERN, 50, and BHAVANI JAROFF, 48, interview their father, KEN MORGANSTERN, 81

RECORDED IN NEW YORK, NEW YORK

Priya Morganstern and Bhavani Jaroff brought in their father, Ken Morganstern, to capture his memories before they slipped away. They came to StoryCorps as a part of our Memory Loss Initiative, a special project to collect stories of people suffering from memory loss.

Ken was diagnosed with Alzheimer's disease about six years ago. In the years since, his memory has grown progressively worse. In the StoryCorps booth, Priya and Bhavani asked him to remember the important experiences of his lifetime—falling in love, marriage and children.

At times, he answers firmly; other times he falters. When Priya asks Ken his age, he answers, "I think eighty-one." At one point, Ken forgets the name of his son, David, but Priya lets him know that she knows certain details of his life might not be available to him: "You'll answer them the best you can from your memory."

In the end, what remains is love. Bhavani pays tribute to her father at the end of the interview, telling him, "You've created such love around you and we want to be with you." Ken answers with fatherly affection, "Thank you, honey. That's awfully nice to hear."

A letter from a listener:

.   .   .

Priya and Bhavani,

Thank you for sharing your interview. I listened to it twice this morning. While I get plenty of support from other daughters of parents with Alzheimer's, something about hearing Ken's voice struck close to the bone. He sounds just like my mom, in ways I can't put into words just now. You have deepened my understanding that my family is far from alone in facing this disease.

.   .   .

February 19, 2006

10. MICHAEL WOLMETZ, 25, interviewed by his girlfriend, DEBORA BRAKARZ, 26

RECORDED IN NEW YORK, NEW YORK

When Michael Wolmetz brought Debora Brakarz to the StoryCorps booth in Grand Central Terminal, she didn't know what the next hour would bring. Michael and Debora had been dating for three months at the time. Debora asked Michael the important questions: "So what was the most emotionally painful thing that ever happened to you?" Michael told Debora the story of unexpectedly losing his father at the age of twenty-two. As he paid tribute to his father, who had been his closest friend, he rustled around in his pocket and pulled out a ring. "So this is the ring that my father gave to my mother. . . . And he saved up and he purchased this and he proposed to my mother with this and so I thought that I would give it to you so he could be with us for this also." He then asks the question: "Will you please marry me?" Through tears, Debora answers with "Yes," "Of course" and "I love you." Michael ends by addressing future generations: "So, kids, this is how your mother and I got married in a booth in Grand Central Station with my father's ring. My grandfather

 was a cab driver for forty years and used to pick people up here every day so it seems right."

Michael Wolmetz and Debora Brakarz got married in the summer of 2005.

January 10, 2004

Visit *www.storycorps.net* to:

- Listen to more stories; share them with others
- Subscribe to our podcast
- Find out how to bring StoryCorps to your community
- Support StoryCorps and help us to continue in our mission

THE CONVERSATION OF A LIFETIME

We encourage you to participate in StoryCorps. Please visit our Web site, www.storycorps.net, to learn about the locations of our StoryBooths across the country. We also have two permanent facilities open year-round in Manhattan. Come visit New York City, make an appointment and record your loved one's voice for history.

If you want to record an interview but are not able to visit one of our StoryBooths, we encourage you to do-it-yourself. Conduct your own interview and ask the questions you've always wanted to ask. You may well be surprised by the power of the experience.

Here's how:

1. Pick a Storyteller

Start the process by figuring out whom you want to interview. A grandparent? An old friend? Your mom? The person you invite might be hesitant. "I don't have much to talk about," he'll say, or, "You already know everything about my life." Remind your friend, your mother—whoever it is—how important you think their story is and how valuable it will be to future generations. Let that person know you would be honored to record his story.

2. Create a Question List

No matter how well you know your storyteller, a little preparation will improve the quality of your interview enormously. What would you like to learn from that person? We've designed a question generator to make preparing questions a little easier. You can find it at www.storycorps.net.

Here are some questions that have yielded great responses:

- What have you learned in life?
- What does your future hold?
- What are you most proud of?
- Do you have any regrets?
- What was the happiest moment of your life? The saddest?
- Is there something about yourself that you think no one knows?
- How would you like to be remembered?

We've also found that at the end of a session it can be powerful to turn the tables and tell the person you're interviewing what she means to you. In the back of this book, you can find many more questions.

3. Purchase or Borrow Recording Equipment (and Get Comfortable with It)

It is not difficult to make a terrific and clear recording of someone's voice. We strongly suggest that you create a recording with the best sound quality possible—it's much more enjoyable and easy to listen to and will be appreciated by future generations. You will need three pieces of equipment: a recording device, a microphone and headphones. (You can learn more about equipment options at our Web site.) The recording equipment can be as simple as a micro cassette recorder or basic digital voice recorder, a pair of headphones and an inexpensive microphone (handheld, not clip-on). You can find both basic and more sophisticated recording equipment at your local electronics store. (StoryCorps also has a small equipment loan program called StoryKits, which you can also learn about at our Web site.) Whatever equipment you choose, we strongly suggest that you practice using your equipment before you sit down for your interview.

A few things to remember:

- It's best to always wear headphones when recording. Your headphones are your "ears" for the interview; they tell you exactly what you'll hear on your finished recording. Use them to adjust the microphone position so the sound is as clear as possible.
- Hold the microphone close, about one spread-out hand's length from your storyteller's mouth. Always hold the microphone in your hand, moving it between you and your storyteller.
- Be careful of microphone noise. The low rumbling sound you hear when you move the microphone in your hands is known as "mic-handling noise." You can avoid it by using a light touch and not shifting around too much. If you need to move the microphone, make sure to wait until your storyteller has finished speaking.

You may want to get together a group of friends and purchase recording equipment together. Someone from the group can act as the "engineer" during your interview and operate the equipment so you can focus on asking the questions. You can also share and talk about the stories you've recorded with the group.

4. Choose an Interview Location

Pick the quietest place possible. A carpeted living room or bedroom is often best. Avoid large empty rooms and kitchens, which are filled with reflective surfaces and appliance noise.

We try to make the inside of each StoryCorps booth something of a sacred space, as peaceful and serene as possible. You may want to do the same: turn the lights low. Do whatever you can to make you and your subject as comfortable as possible.

Prevent noisy distractions. Close the door; unplug the phone; turn off your cell phone. Turn off anything that is making noise: buzzing fluorescent lights, air conditioners, fans. Listen for noise during the interview as well. If your storyteller fiddles with her necklace, for example, feel free to let her know it's making noise. Never record interviews with a radio or television on in the background.

5. Set Up and Test the Equipment

Set up your equipment as early as possible and make sure you're comfortable with it. This way you'll be able to focus on the person you are interviewing and not the equipment. Before you begin your interview, record your storyteller answering a few warm-up questions such as "Can you describe what this room looks like?" or, "Tell me what you had for breakfast." Stop, rewind and listen to the recording you just made to make sure everything is working. Remember to press RECORD again when you start the interview for real.

6. Begin the Conversation

Start your interview by stating your name, your age, the date and the location of the interview. For example, "My name is Annie Smith. I'm forty-one years old. The date is November 23, 2008, and I'm sitting with my grandfather Mark Smith in his living room in Hannibal, Missouri." Now ask your storyteller to state the same information.

Use your question list. Remember, the questions you write in advance are just suggestions. Trust your instincts. If something interests you or merits further exploration, ask more questions. Sometimes your storyteller will need "permission" to talk about a certain topic. Granting that permission might be as easy as saying, "Tell me more."

Don't let the question list constrain you. Feel free to ask questions in whatever order feels right. Take breaks if your storyteller needs them.

Try not to say "uh huh" or interrupt when something interesting or important is being said. You can always use visual cues like nodding your head when you want to encourage the storyteller to keep going.

7. Get Great Stories

Here are some tips for helping the conversation flow:

Listen closely. Look at your storyteller's eyes, not the mic. Nod your head. Smile. Stay interested and engaged.

Be yourself. You can laugh with the person you are interviewing or even cry with him. Real moments are the best moments.

Stick with the good stuff. When you hear something that moves you, feel free to talk about it more. If the current topic isn't what you wanted to put on tape, gently steer the conversation back on course.

Ask emotional questions. Questions such as "How does this make you feel?" often elicit interesting responses. Don't be afraid to ask.

Respect your subject. If there's a topic she just doesn't want to talk about, respect her wishes and move on.

Take notes during the interview. Write down any questions or stories you might want to return to later in your interview.

Be curious and honest and keep an open heart. Great things will happen.

8. Wrap It Up

Before you turn off your recorder, do two things: ask the storyteller if there is anything else that she wants to talk about and thank her. Sharing a story can be difficult for some people. It's a privilege to have someone share her story with you. Express your gratitude.

If you have a digital camera, take a picture of your interviewee against a plain background (or, if there's someone else around, have him take a picture of the two of you) in the style of the StoryCorps pictures you find in this book.

Make sure to label your recordings properly, make copies for relatives and friends and store them in a safe place so they'll be available for generations to come. (Unfortunately, StoryCorps does not have the capacity at the present time to enter these do-it-yourself interviews into our archives.)

9. Share the Conversation

The conversation doesn't have to end once you turn off your recorder. In fact, it may just be the beginning.

With the permission of your storyteller, you might share the interview by making copies of your recording to give to family and friends. You might also host a listening party. Invite others to your home to listen to your recording and share a conversation afterward. You could also listen to StoryCorps stories on our Web site.

10. Plant a Seed

Storytelling can be a powerful tool, and your imagination is really the limit of what you can do with it. If you are a teacher, for instance, you might consider playing clips in your classroom as part of a history or writing unit. If you are part of a mentoring program, you could interview your mentor or mentee about their life experiences.

Use the checklist and questions that follow to make sharing stories a part of your family, community or working life.

Congratulations!
You have just joined the StoryCorps revolution!

DO-IT-YOURSELF
CHECKLIST

Things to Bring to the Interview

- Your question list
- Recording device
- Microphone
- Headphones
- Extra batteries and tapes
- Pen or pencil

Before You Begin Your Interview

- Find the quietest place possible to record.
- Turn off radios and TVs and move away from noisy appliances like refrigerators and clocks.
- Make sure you and your storyteller are comfortable.
- Do a test recording, holding the microphone about one spread-out hand's distance from your storyteller's mouth. If anything sounds strange, stop and figure out what the problem is before starting the interview.

During Your Interview

- Double-check that the recorder is actually recording (not on PAUSE).
- Start each tape with an ID: State your name, your age, the date and the location of the interview. Ask your storyteller to state the same information.

- Don't say "Uh huh" when your subject is talking. Instead, nod your head.
- Ask emotional questions such as "How did this make you feel?"
- Look your storyteller in the eyes and stay engaged.
- Respect your subject always.
- Don't be afraid to stick with amazing moments in the interview—if you hear something you're interested in, ask follow-up questions.
- Be curious and keep an open heart. Great things will happen.

When You Finish

- If you recorded the interview on tape, label it. Store the tapes in a cool place out of direct sunlight.

FAVORITE STORYCORPS QUESTIONS

General

- What are the most important lessons you've learned in life?
- What are you most proud of?
- What was the happiest moment of your life? The saddest?
- Is there something about yourself that you think no one knows?
- How would you like to be remembered?
- Is there anything we didn't talk about that you would like to add?

Childhood and Family

- When and where were you born?
- Where did you grow up and what was it like?
- Tell me about your parents.
- Did you get into trouble? What was the worst thing you did?
- Do you have any siblings? What were they like growing up?
- What did you look like?
- How would you describe yourself as a child? Were you happy?
- What is your best memory of childhood? Worst?
- Did you have a nickname? How'd you get it?
- Who were your best friends? What were they like?
- How would you describe a perfect day when you were young?
- What did you think your life would be like when you were older?
- Can you tell me some classic stories from your childhood?

School and Education

- What are your best memories of grade school/high school/college/graduate school? Worst memories?
- What kind of student were you?
- What would you do for fun?
- How would your classmates remember you?
- Was there a teacher or teachers who had a particularly strong influence on your life? Tell me about them.
- Do you have any other favorite stories from school?

Love and Romance

- Do you have a love of your life?
- When did you first fall in love?
- Can you tell me about your first kiss?
- What was your first serious relationship?
- What lessons have you learned from your relationships?

Marriage and Commitment

- How did you meet your husband/wife?
- How did you know he/she was "the one"?
- How did you propose?
- What were the best times? The most difficult times?
- Did you ever get divorced? Can you tell me about it?
- What advice do you have for young couples?
- Do you have any favorite stories from your marriage or about your husband/wife?

Parenthood

- When did you first find out that you'd be a parent? How did you feel?
- Can you describe the moment when you saw your child for the first time?

- How has being a parent changed you?
- What are your dreams for your children?
- Do you remember when your last child left home for good?
- Do you have any favorite stories about your kids?

Work

- What do you do for a living?
- Tell me about how you got into your line of work.
- Do you like your job?
- What did you want to be when you grew up?
- What lessons has your work life taught you?
- Do you plan on retiring? If so, when? How do you feel about it?
- Do you have any favorite stories from your work life?

Religion and Spirituality

- Can you tell me about your religious beliefs/spiritual beliefs?
- What is your religion?
- Have you experienced any miracles?
- What was the most profound spiritual moment of your life?
- Do you believe in an afterlife? What do you think it will be like?
- When you meet God, what would you want to say to Him?

Ethnicity and Family Heritage

- What is your ethnic background?
- Where is your mom's family from? Where is your dad's family from?
- What traditions have been passed down in your family?
- Who were your favorite relatives? Can you tell me any stories about them?
- Do you remember any of the stories they used to tell you?
- What are the classic family stories? Jokes? Songs?

War and Service

- Were you in the military?
- Did you go to war? What was it like?
- How did war change you?
- During your service, can you recall times when you were afraid?
- What are your strongest memories from your time in the military?
- What lessons did you learn from this time in your life?

Illness

- Can you tell me about your illness?
- Do you think about dying?
- Are you scared?
- How do you imagine your death?
- Do you believe in an afterlife?
- Do you regret anything?
- Do you look at your life differently now from before you were diagnosed?
- Do you have any last wishes?
- If you were to give advice to me or my children, or even children to come in our family, what would it be?
- What are the most important things you've learned from life?
- Has this illness changed you? What have you learned?
- How do you want to be remembered?

CREDITS

. . .

PRODUCER: *Michael Garofalo*
EDITOR: *Sarah Kramer*
NARRATOR: *Dave Isay*
LINER NOTES: *Lizzie Jacobs*
MUSIC: *Pullman, courtesy of Thrill Jockey Records*
"Two Parts Water," "So Breaks Yesterday,"
"Sunday Morning Traffic," "Tall Grass" and "To Hold Down
a Shadow" from *Turnstyles and Junkpiles*; "Felucca,"
"Same Grain with New Wood," "Forty Fingers"
and "Brewster Road" from *Viewfinder*.

Thank you to all of the participants for lending us
their voices and their stories to make this CD possible.